FAIRACRES PUBLICATIONS 12

LEARNING
TO
PRAY

Mother Mary Clare slg

© 2025 SLG Press
First edition 1970
Second revised edition 2006
Third revised edition 2025

Fairacres Publications 12

ISBN 978-0-7283-0417-8
Fairacres Publications Series ISSN 0307-1405

SLG Press asserts the right of Mother Mary Clare to be identified as the author of this work, in accordance with the Copyright Designs and Patents act, 1988.

All rights reserved. No part of this publication may be reproduced, stored in a retrieval system, or transmitted, in any form or by any means, electronic, mechanical, photocopying, recording or otherwise, without the prior permission of the copyright owner.

ACKNOWLEDGEMENTS
SLG Press is grateful to the following publishers for permission to reprint copyright material: to Gill & Macmillan Ltd for 'The Telephone' and 'Lord I have Time' (excerpt), in *Prayers of Life* by Michel Quoist. And to Sheed & Ward, an imprint of Rowman & Littlefield Publishing Inc., for permission to reprint the same material from *Prayers* by Michel Quoist for sale and distribution in USA and Canada.

Edited and typeset in Palatino Linotype by Julia Craig-McFeely

Biblical quotations are taken from the New Revised Standard Version of the Bible unless otherwise noted.

Cover image by Sister Rosemary SLG

SLG Press
Convent of the Incarnation
Fairacres • Oxford
www.slgpress.co.uk

Printed by
Grosvenor Group Ltd, Loughton, Essex

CONTENTS

Learning to Pray — 1
   Why Pray? — 2
   Prayer as part of redemptive action — 2
   Prayer must be God's activity in us — 4
   Purity of heart — conversion of life — 5
   Use of creative faculties in early stages of prayer — 9
   The night of faith — 9
   Prayer brings in the power of God — 12

Prayer — a love affair with God — 15
   Listening prayer — 16
   Attentive silence — 18
   Relaxation as preparation for prayer — 20
   Rhythmic prayer — 22
   The use of time — 23
   What holds us back? — 24
   Definition of contemplation — 25
   Result of contemplation — 26

The End at which we Aim — 27
   Union with God in love — 27
   The underlying spiritual conflict — 28

LEARNING

TO PRAY

Learning to Pray

Prayer is the gateway to the vision of God for which we were created. It is the means of free and conscious intercourse between the creature and the Creator, and it expresses the union between the two. It is the art of spiritual living and will be incomplete if it includes only the art of the practice of the presence of God, without the necessary complement of the practice of our own presence.

Some words from the Collects for the third and seventh Sundays after Trinity (Book of Common Prayer) can be taken as signposts to the general theme of learning to pray:

> O Lord, we beseech thee mercifully to hear us, and grant that we to whom *thou hast given a hearty desire to pray* ...

and,

> Lord of all power and might, who art the author and giver of all good things,
> *graft* in our hearts the love of thy Name,
> *increase* in us true religion,
> *nourish* us with all goodness and of thy great mercy
> *keep* us in the same ...through Jesus Christ our Lord.
>   Amen.

These well-known prayers from the liturgy after Trinity should bring us up sharp with the awareness that this *hearty desire to pray* is not something we can take for granted, and that the very fact of praying at all is a gift of God, deriving from our incorporation into Christ's prayer; a gift which he must increase and nourish so that we may be kept by the Holy Spirit in perseverance and stability in order to progress in prayer.

In fact, we must have the right dispositions and attitudes of body, mind and spirit in order to pray.

Why pray?

I want first to turn the title of this book into a challenging question. Do we really desire to pray? We must always be aware of the increasing pressure of our present day humanistic, if not promiscuous, society which will say, *Why pray at all? Would it not be better to meet and serve Christ in my brother and sister and bring the Church as a whole, and the Religious Life in particular, into the suffering world by a deeply God-centred and consecrated activity?* Many would surely say that this alone is what makes prayer relevant today.

Prayer as part of redemptive action

First and foremost, therefore, we must try to dispel this entirely false dichotomy between prayer as a purely Godward or personal activity on the one hand, and on the other as a compassionate involvement with the world's pain, insecurity and frustration which would seem to make 'prayer' in the old traditional sense irrelevant. No one has expressed the truth of the real activity of praying better than Thomas Merton in an article which he was in the process of revising just before he died, and which is as true for all committed Christians as for monks and nuns. He writes:

> This age, that by its very nature is a time of crisis and of revolution and of struggle, calls for the special searching and questioning which is the work of the monk in his silence, his meditation and his prayer. For the monk searches not only his own heart, he plunges deep into the heart of the world of which he remains a part, although he seems to have 'left it'.[1]

---

[1] Thomas Merton, *The Climate of Monastic Prayer* (Cistercian Publications, 1969; Liturgical Press, 2018).

This touches very deeply the whole concept of the coinherence of humanity and of the cosmic unity into which prayer leads us, and of which silence is a necessary accompaniment. Merton continues:

> In reality the monk withdraws from the world only in order to listen more intently to the deepest and most neglected voices that proceed from its inner depths. The way of prayer is not a subtle escape from the Christian economy of the Incarnation and Redemption. It is a special way of following Christ, of sharing in his Passion and Resurrection and in his Redemption of the world.
>
> This is precisely the monk's [the Christian's] chief service to the world, this silence, this questioning, this listening, this humble and courageous exposure to what the world ignores about itself, both good and evil. The monk [the Christian] who is truly a man of prayer, and who seriously faces the challenge of his vocation in all its depth, is by that very fact exposed to the emptiness, to the lack of authenticity, to the quest for fidelity and truth and to the lostness of modern man.

Thomas Merton has here immediately broadened our perspective of prayer, and helped us to see that when we pray we are being united with our Lord in his own redemptive action. We are, moreover, being drawn into the great cosmic battle against evil which is to bring into the here and now of our daily lives the fruits of Christ's victorious Passion.

Seen in this light it would seem strange that we all find it difficult to recognize the urgency of prayer, and yet this is no modern problem. In the Gospel story we see the disciples at the foot of the mount of Transfiguration full of apostolic zeal and awareness that they had been commissioned by the Lord to preach the good news of the Kingdom and heal the sick as well as to cast out devils. But when it came to the crunch, the sick boy was still helpless and was still possessed by strange forces both spiritual and psychic which they were unable to dispel or heal. The occasion was one of tragedy, drawing out the sympathy of the beholders, and heightened because of the expectation of the parents and the disappointment of the disciples themselves at their own incapacity.

On this occasion it was not compassionate involvement that was lacking, but the dynamic power of their prayer: 'However, this kind does not go out except by prayer and fasting' (Matt. 17:21 NKJV). The disciples had been given the Divine Commission and doubtless they had tried to carry out the Lord's wish with all the concentration and force of their natural human energy, but this had been to no avail, for what was in fact needed was the transforming power of prayer.

Prayer must be God's activity in us

The prayer the disciples had to learn was something more than carrying out a command, or seeking the intervention of Divine Power as a magical act. In the case of our Lord, his prayer was the complete expression of the union of his human will and energy with that of his Father. In Jesus, God's activity was central, operating in and through the Divine Humanity without let or hindrance. During our feeble efforts to pray we are constantly confronted by our own imperfect and often very self-expressive human faculties, which get in the way of that simple, complete co-operation with the Spirit of God which is the essence of prayer. It is the prayer of the 'just man made perfect' (Heb. 12:23), that is, of power.

There is another Gospel saying of our Lord about prayer which it is valuable to remember in this context for it is often misunderstood: 'I will do whatever you ask in my name.' (John 14:13). We, in our misplaced optimism, which we all too often confuse with the theological virtue of faith, think that all we have to do is to make our prayer with the concluding invocation, 'Through Jesus Christ our Lord', then all will be well and God will give us the answer we want. If he doesn't we often get confused and dispirited, like the rich young man who could not rise up to the challenge of total commitment, and we tend to say, *There, I knew it wouldn't work*, and then we wipe off prayer as another of those religious techniques which may have had their part to play in years gone by but not in the technological wonderland of the modern age.

The first lesson we have to learn about prayer, therefore, is that it is God's activity in us and not a self-activated process of our own.

> Look well, O soul, upon thyself,
>   lest spiritual ambition
>   should mislead and blind thee
>   to thy essential task—
>   to wait in quietness
>   to knock and persevere in humble faith.
> Knock thou in love, nor fail to keep thy place before the door
>   that when Christ wills—and not before—
>   he shall open unto thee the treasures of his love.
> Grant me humility of soul
>   that I may grow in penitence
>   dependent on the Holy Spirit's light.[2]

Purity of heart—conversion of life

The Desert Fathers, those great masters of the spiritual life, knew all about the essential condition of learning to pray. They called it 'purity of heart', without which there can be no true *metanoia* or conversion, for we only pray if our hearts are truly pure in the sense of our Lord's teaching in the Sermon on the Mount, 'Blessed are the pure in heart for they shall see God.' (Matt. 5:8).

> Most loving Lord, hold thou me fast to live by thee,
>   in all occasions of my life,
>   in the busyness of consciousness
>   and when the physical doth sleep.
> Keep thou my heart united to thyself
>   to be the temple of the Holy Ghost,
>   that he may show me of thyself

---

[2] Fr Gilbert Shaw, *The Face of Love* (SLG Press, 1977), 101.

and be the power of my soul
to be more fully one with thee.
Still thou the inmost depths of memory and will
that all my thinking may return
to know that thou dost hold my heart.
Cleanse thou the complex patterns of unconsciousness
that nothing should control the will
or turn my heart from loving thee,
from serving thee in spirit and in truth,
that every thought and action of the day
may be controlled and rendered to thy praise,
determining both thought and action to thy will,
that while I sleep my heart may wake
rendering unto thee my love
to glorify thy name,
that all that is not wholly reconciled to thee
may be resolved and rectified by love,
the flame which is the knowledge of thyself.[3]

The above is by Gilbert Shaw, one of the greatest of our Anglican spiritual directors. What he is saying in modern language is what was said by the unknown author of the fourteenth-century mystical texts, *The Cloud of Unknowing*, and Walter Hilton's *The Scale of Perfection*, and in the seventeenth century by Father Augustine Baker in *Holy Wisdom*: that there is only one way to learn to pray, and that is by first entering into the cell of self-knowledge and being ready to open all the avenues of our human faculties to the cleansing power of the Holy Spirit.

When the time for prayer comes we all know what it means when our mind, memory and imagination separately and all together seem to be in a state of confusion and over-activity: our bodies are restless and taut, and it is hard to be still for half an hour. We will think about this more in detail later, but for the moment let us take the words of St Simeon the New Theologian, of the Eastern Orthodox tradition, and absorb his teaching when he says:

---

[3] Shaw, *The Face of Love*, 99, slightly adapted.

Where there is deep humility [purity of heart] thither comes the Holy Spirit; when the grace of the worshipful Spirit comes, the man under its influence is filled with all purity. Then he sees God and God too looks on him.[4]

This entering into the 'cell of self-knowledge' brings us first of all up against the fact that prayer and daily life are indivisible: I must learn to pray as I am, and accept myself as I am, and not as the ideal praying person that perhaps I would like to imagine myself to be. In other words, we must grow to understand ourselves and realize that it is when our natural passions are most active, our minds most distracted, that we must grow to accept ourselves as real persons, and offer ourselves to God in prayer at this point of tension.

At the beginning of our learning to pray, therefore, we must relate prayer to conversion of life. One is relatively useless without the other; and prayer which is the fruit of true conversion is an activity, an adventure, and sometimes a dangerous one because at times it brings neither peace nor comfort, but challenge, conflict and new responsibility.

That is why so many old ways of prayer and books about prayer and meditation may seem to have 'gone dead on us', because, subconsciously at least, when we were using them we were hoping to get something for ourselves from prayer, at least a sense of security, and at best a growing sensible realization and knowledge of God; instead of grasping that the essential heart of prayer is the throwing away of ourselves in complete self-oblation to God, so that he can do with us what he wills. Any form of prayer which does not stimulate love to give all we have and are, soon becomes dry and sterile, merely a formal duty.

In the great tradition of Christian prayer, true praying is to stand naked before God as a creature before our Creator and as a penitent before our Saviour. This brings with it a growing awareness

---

[4] Quoted in David G. R. Keller, *Oasis of Wisdom: The Worlds of the Desert Fathers and Mothers* (Liturgical Press, 2005), 143.

of the Majesty of God and a growing realization of our utter nothingness before him. That is why all the great Saints have genuinely believed themselves to be the greatest of sinners.

'My God if you exist, make me know you', exclaimed Charles de Foucauld before his conversion,[5] and how often that is a reflection of our own inner longing for God as we gradually waken to the fact that without him we are nothing. When this happens, instead of thinking that everything must have gone wrong with our prayer, we must believe it is a real sign of growth in stability and maturity. It is a cause for great thanksgiving when we are prepared to make that leap of faith at the call of God into a way of prayer that may seem dark and meaningless but which, in effect, is an invitation of love to greater intimacy, though we ourselves may be aware of nothing except our inability to formulate our deepest longings.

Here we must be childlike and believe that God does know the inner secrets of our hearts, and that there is no need for us to formulate them in words. At the same time we should have the times of prayer in which we must do something. If formal meditation is impossible at this time, and it probably will be, we must just try to make some simple, short and, if possible, spontaneous acts of faith, hope and love, thanksgiving and offering, in order to anchor ourselves and not drift on the one hand into self-centred depression, or on the other in the opposite direction, into a *wrong* form of what St Teresa of Ávila called 'the prayer of quiet'.[6] That great Saint and Doctor of the Church, constantly reminded her nuns that there is no true way of prayer except through growing union with our Lord Incarnate, and this is not incompatible with the darkness of the senses and the spirit at which I have just hinted, which must come to all of us if we are earnest in prayer, and which

---

[5] 'Mon Dieu si vous existez, faites que je vous connaisse', trans. in Jean François Six, *Spiritual Autobiography of Charles of Foucauld* (P. J. Kenedy, 1964), 15.

[6] *Teresa of Ávila: The Book of Her Life*, 14.1, trans. Kieran Kavanaugh OCD and Otilio Rodriguez OCD (Hackett Publishing Company, 2008), 81.

is, of course, what the great books of St John of the Cross on mystical prayer are all about.[7]

Use of creative faculties in early stages of prayer

In the early days of learning to practise what used to be called formal meditation it is perfectly right that we should use our natural creative gifts as part of our learning to pray, provided they are seen as means to an end and not an end in themselves, or for our natural enjoyment. For example, some may be encouraged to use their love of poetry to express their desire for God in prayer, writing prose or verse. Another with artistic gifts may have the opportunity to learn to paint in order more particularly to direct art and prayer into one unity. Others may find real inspiration in using reproductions of the old masters to relate the beauty of visual form to biblical and other spiritual writings in order to stimulate their affective acts of prayer.

The night of faith

But all this must be seen as a stage on the way by which the Holy Spirit leads us into the night of faith and begins to strip the soul of all dependency on natural aids to prayer. We must be ready to give up these prayerful activities and lay ourselves open to a deeper degree of purification of the faculties—a stage when it will largely seem to us that we are doing nothing—to prepare us for the transition from activity to passivity in prayer as God's way of preparing us to *be* rather than to *make* acts of love.

---

[7] John of the Cross (1542–1591) wrote a number of treatises including the *Ascent of Mount Carmel* (c. 1583), about the soul seeking union with God, but the best known are his poetic works, the *Dark Night of the Soul* (c. 1579) and the *Spiritual Canticle* (after 1582). His writings are available online at the Christian Classics Ethereal Library, www.ccel.org/ccel/john_cross (accessed 13 March 2025).

We are being led to perceive things as a whole in relation to their final end and the will of God, and this is an enrichment both of knowledge and of energy. It is an enrichment of knowledge as our eyes are opened to see things as they are in the sight of God and in their true effect as they are related to others; and it is an enrichment of energy as our prayer is directed to one end, namely that all may be reconciled to God in the judgement, so that the energizing life and love of God is condensed into one channel and therefore its generating power is increased. Instead of dissipating our knowledge and the energy of God's healing power by passing feverishly from one point to another and trying to work out ways and means, we lift up all into the will and purpose of God.

I would like to draw your attention to the spiritual letters of Dom John Chapman OSB (1865–1933), Abbot of Downside from 1929 until his death. He underlines what I have tried to express, that some form of the night of the senses is common to everyone and that the widespread assumption that prayer will bring much sensible consolation is extremely misleading. He advises one of his penitents:

> We must aim at being in the desert and not at any consciousness of God's grace. One is inclined to say, 'I am so weak I cannot go on like this', but God knows best. Make up your mind once and for all that dryness is best and you will find you are frightened of having anything else.[8]

In other words, which perhaps some of us understand more easily, we might say that the agony of frustration which many learners of prayer feel, and which I certainly tend to feel when confronted with very many books with titles such as 'How to Pray', is analogous to the sort of anguish a thirsty man feels if given an extract from a chemistry textbook on water and its properties, when all he is longing for is a glass of water to drink.

---

[8] Dom Roger Hudleston OSB, ed., *The Spiritual Letters of Dom John Chapman, O.S.B. Fourth Abbot of Downside* (Sheed and Ward, 1935), 173.

If, instead of following our formal meditations—our schemes and techniques which we have all, at one time or another, had to practise, and rightly so—we could realize the inner meaning of such words as 'Jesus is prayer', I believe much of this thirst and our own sense of hopelessness and inability to pray would be quenched with the living water of God's love, whether we were aware of it or not. Something of which we have rather lost sight in much of our current thinking about prayer is just this need, and it is expressed in the hymn, 'Tell me the old, old story of Jesus and his love'.

> Tell me the old, old story
> Of unseen things above,
> Of Jesus and His glory,
> Of Jesus and His love.
> Tell me the story simply,
> As to a little child,
> For I am weak and weary,
> And helpless and defiled
>
> Tell me the story slowly,
> That I may take it in,
> That wonderful redemption,
> God's remedy for sin.
> Tell me the story often,
> For I forget so soon;
> The early dew of morning
> Has passed away at noon.
>
> Tell me the story softly,
> With earnest tones and grave;
> Remember I'm the sinner
> Whom Jesus came to save.
> Tell me the story always,
> If you would really be,
> In any time of trouble,
> A comforter to me.

> Tell me the same old story
> When you have cause to fear
> That this world's empty glory
> Is costing me too dear.
> Yes, and when that world's glory
> Is dawning on my soul,
> Tell me the old, old story:
> Christ Jesus makes thee whole.[9]

To set us praying, many of us need to relate our desire for God, for what God is and what he does in Jesus, as expressed in our 'private prayer' to our participation in the Eucharist and other corporate acts of worship, where we are all drawn into and become part of the mighty redemptive acts of God. One of the dangers of the past has been the dichotomy between private and liturgical prayer, whereas in reality they complement each other. One of the unspoken benefits which all Christians can participate if they will, is the constant hearing of the 'old, old story' through the words and actions of corporate worship; if only we would wake up and listen. Listening in prayer is very important, and we shall think more about that later.

Prayer brings in the power of God

We must see all this against the background of the inalienable purposes of God and the eternal mysteries of the faith, and realize that the world will not be brought back to an acknowledgment of the power of Christ unless those who represent the praying heart of the Church, have indeed prayed back the Cross and its message of love into the centre of Christian witness. 'And I, when I am lifted up from the earth, will draw all people to myself.' (John 12:32). By the generosity of our living witness as we seek in prayer to be drawn into deeper union with our Lord in his Passion, we shall be

---

[9] Originally a poem written in 1866 by Katherine Hankey (1804–1911), set to music by William Howard Doane (1832–1915).

giving ourselves to be participators in his continuous intercession to draw us and all humankind into unity and into the knowledge of himself.

Prayer as union with God is the primary means of bringing in the power of the love of God to expose, judge and correct the misuse of power: in the words of St John of the Cross, 'To put love in where love is not'.[10] Through the act of God in taking manhood into the Godhead, the whole of human energy has been redirected into his perfect offering, and the spiritual powers that would enslave us have been overcome. It is not through forcing the human will but through drawing it to recognize and co-operate with the power of God expressed in love that we bear witness to the power of redeeming love. It is through lives offered in union with Christ's intercessory prayer that the energy of the power of God is both generated and set free for the reversal of evil.

What has been said so far may be summed up as follows:

The Holy Spirit is the initiator of all prayer, which is a gift from God.

We must be prepared to pay the cost of having the ground of our souls prepared for God's action. Think of the parable of the sower in this context (Matt. 13:3–8; Mark 4:3–20; Luke 8:5–8).

This preparation will entail long periods when our faith and fidelity will be tested to the utmost both in prayer and in daily life, for we cannot separate the two.

All our prayer activities must be seen as means and not ends in themselves, because they are to lead us to the familiar friendship with Jesus which Thomas à Kempis expresses so well in The Imitation of Christ 'If you truly desire a life of prayer, the way to get it is by praying':

---

[10] Letter 26, Madrid 6 July 1591, to Madre María de la Encarnación in Segovia, in *The Collected Works of Saint John of the Cross*, trans. Kieran Kavanaugh OCD and Otilio Rodriguez OCD (ICS Publications, 1991), 22.

Love Him and keep him for thy friend, who when all go away will not forsake thee, nor suffer thee to perish in the end. Some time or other thou must be separated from all, whether thou wilt or no. Keep close to Jesus both in life and in death, and commit thyself unto His faithfulness, who when all fail can alone help thee.[11]

As Thomas Merton tells us:

> ... In prayer we discover what we already have through the indwelling Spirit of God and our incorporation through Baptism into Christ. You start where you are and you deepen what you already have. Everything has been given to us in Christ. All we need is to experience what we already possess.[12]

---

[11] Thomas à Kempis, *The Imitation of Christ*, bk II, cap. 7.2, modern edition (Ignatius Press, 2004).

[12] Thomas Merton, *The Monastic Journey* (Cistercian Publications, 1992), 55.

Prayer—a love affair with God

> Look graciously upon us, O Holy Spirit of God, and give us for our hallowing, thoughts which pass into prayer, prayer which passes into love, and love which passes into life eternal lived with you.
>
> *Eric Milner-White (1884–1963)*[13]

Prayer is essentially a love affair with God, not schemes or techniques or ways of prayer, but the most direct open approach of each one of us as a person to God our Creator, Redeemer and Sanctifier—beyond all methods or ideas. Therefore we should implore the Holy Spirit to teach us, for as St Paul reminds us, he prays within us—he is our director.[14] We must be absolutely confident that he will bring us to the desired goal if we are prepared to pay the cost because God's love is always drawing us to himself. He draws: we respond—'Draw me, we will run after thee' (Song 1:4 KJV); 'We love because he first loved us' (1 John 4:19).

Above everything else, let us be clear that what we are seeking in prayer is God himself: not thoughts about him or about ourselves in relation to him. Years ago I read a life of a Carmelite nun who was Prioress of the Carmel in Dijon shortly before Elizabeth of the Trinity went there in 1901. She says about prayer:

> In coming to prayer you must put yourself in the presence not of something [*non de quelque chose*] but of Someone [*mais de Quelqu'un*]; you have confrontation not with an idea, you are face to face with a living being who listens to you, speaks to you and prepares to give you everything. In fact you stand face to face with the living God [*face au Dieu vivant*].[15]

---

[13] Eric Milner-White, *A Cambridge Bede Book* (Longmans, Green & Co., 1936).
[14] Cf. Romans 8:9–11.
[15] Cited in Lucia de Gasperi and Alcide de Gasperi, *Appunti spirituali e lettere al padre* (Morcellian, 1969).

To stand before the living God, what an adventure! To stand face to face before the living God, not in a vague way in a place we call heaven, but in the here and now of our moment to moment living, by, with and in Christ, as we are made part of his prayer and his offering to the Father through the power of the Holy Spirit.

Father Richard Meux Benson SSJE, founder of The Mission Priests of St John the Evangelist says,

> The soul in its littleness looks upon God in his greatness and loves him; and God in his infinity gazes upon the individual soul in its littleness, and loves it.[16]

Prayer, then, is a love affair and that entails *dialogue*. There is always a danger that we may seem to have so many prayerful obligations to fulfil that this aspect gets overlaid. Even Mass and our daily prayers such as the Divine Office can at times become very much a duty to be performed.

We have to turn that boredom into love and sacrificial offering. And perhaps all the countless opportunities of learning the lessons of praying love may be thought of as equivalent to the interminable letters and phone calls that happen before any permanent relationship is established in the initial stages of a love affair. The important thing is that these times of communication must not be mistaken for the engagement itself, or for the final oblation of each to the other in the fullness of love.

Listening prayer

When one really loves, the words become less important and listening brings deeper awareness and greater sensitivity to the meaning of love. This is what I meant earlier by listening prayer. It is part of the great necessity there is to deepen our silence, certainly interiorly, and possibly exteriorly also, and it marks the transition from the

---

[16] Richard Meux Benson, *Instructions on the Religious Life: Third Series* (Mowbray, 1951), 140.

more active forms of prayer, such as meditation or affective prayer, to the quieter and more receptive contemplative prayer.

Saint Paul says, 'these things God has revealed to us through the Spirit; for the Spirit searches everything, even the depths of God.' (1 Cor. 2:10). To hear these 'deep' things we need to be still and listen. The positive aspect of silence cannot be too much stressed for it is little understood. As the Sisters of the Love of God are reminded in their Rule, the spirit of silence must be faithfully cultivated,

> for it prepares the way for the union of the soul with the will of God and is an offering of perpetual reverence to his majesty ... it should be remembered that silence must cover all the levels of the conscious life; there must be an outward silence of speech and movement, a silence of the mind for the overcoming of vain imaginations and distractions, and a silence of the soul in the surrender of the will to be still and know that God is God, leading to a silence of spirit, which is the preparation for the fullness of contemplation.

The Rule continues very practically, and tells us that silence can be broken not only by speech and hurried unrecollected movement, but also by idle curiosity, for it is in stillness that all our being is trained for deeper recollection.

Probably that word 'recollection' is one about which we have all had difficulty from time to time. We tend to think that we should try to have the conscious awareness of God continually in our minds, and this is, of course, impossible if we are to do our work conscientiously and thoughtfully. Obviously recollection should mean rather that we have a lively sense of *realizing* what it is we are doing wherever we are, whether at Mass, teaching, attending classes, at work, travelling, looking after others; all our activity is directed to the one centre, God, out of which and into which all our prayer and loving service flows. In other words recollection is a sensitive awareness that everything we think or touch has God as its centre.

Attentive silence

What does this mean in relation to our prayer? A relationship can be stunted and actually become very boring if one or other participant keeps up a continuous monologue. If prayer is a relationship with God let us not be afraid of being silent, for it is in silence that God will reveal to us the riches of his love. As we shall see shortly, it must be a listening, attentive silence or otherwise prayer time may become a sleep time! To quote again from Thomas Merton:

> The religious in his silence, his meditation and prayer searches not only his own heart but plunges deep into the heart of the world of which he remains a part although he seems to have left it …. He withdraws in order to listen more intently to the deepest and most neglected voices that proceed from its inner depths.[17]

This is the real meaning of intercession; not telling God in your own words of the needs and sorrows of the world, but through your own silent attentive spirit focussing the love of God where the need is greatest.

Silence, therefore, is the doorway through which we pass to a deeper understanding of Christ's prayer for the world, and we must not be afraid to feel within ourselves some of those violent passions and fears that we believe prayer will bring to Christ's reconciliation. As Christians we must not try to escape the burden of sharing in the sorrows of humanity. 'No man is an island', as John Donne reminds us, and today the whole principle of coinherence, of which the books of Charles Williams are vivid examples, brings this truth home to us in a very realistic and inescapable way.[18] This kind of

---

[17] Thomas Merton, *Contemplative Prayer* (Darton, Longman and Todd, 1973), 25.
[18] *Outlines of Romantic Theology*, ed. Alice Mary Hadfield (1924, publ. posthumously, Eerdmans, 1990); *Descent into Hell* (Faber & Faber, 1937); *He Came Down From Heaven* (Heinemann, 1938); *The Descent of the Dove* (Longmans, 1939); *Religion and Love in Dante: The Theology of Romantic Love* (Dacre Press, 1941); *The Way of Exchange* (James Clarke, 1941).

prayer is both costly and a privilege, for as we learn to see our part in this burden of humanity's sin, something of the prayer of Christ is re-enacted in us. As Fr Maurice Villain says in a meditation on the High Priestly Prayer of Christ, we must be 'the welcoming milieu in which this prayer can continue to reverberate.'[19] Can we therefore afford to neglect either silence or listening, which are both instruments to enable our Lord to pray freely in us?

We cannot have this silence if we let ourselves remain on the top level of awareness and activity and so lose the dimension of being in Christ's prayer and reconciliation. Listening is a real ingredient of silence. In the modern rush of the world today we all know the difficulty when we stop talking of getting back 'into the silence'. The mind continues to work and fastens on to the trivialities, our emotions play up in one way or another, our will is struggling for or against some aspect of self. The silence we need to aim at as a starting point is something which seems to be a contradiction, for we must be on the one hand completely alert, and on the other equally relaxed and at rest.

Before I leave this question of listening-silence let me offer one of my favourite prayers from Michel Quoist in his book *Prayers of Life:*

> I have just hung up; why did he telephone?
> I don't know ... Oh! I get it ...
> I talked a lot and listened very little.
>
> Forgive me, Lord, it was a monologue and not a dialogue.
> I explained my idea and did not get his;
> Since I didn't listen, I learned nothing.
> Since I didn't listen, I didn't help.
> Since I didn't listen, we didn't communicate.
>
> Forgive me, Lord, for we were connected,
> And now we are cut off.[20]

---

[19] Fr Maurice Villain SM, 'The High Priestly Prayer', *One in Christ*, vol. 5 (1969), 7.
[20] Michel Quoist, *Prayers* (Sheed and Ward, 1963), 19.

It is not only our own personal relationship with God that will be diminished by lack of silence, but perhaps our failure or over-talkativeness will have cut off direct communication between God and someone else. This is part of the cost and challenge of coinherence. Our dissipation of mind, our instability and lack of courage to face ourselves or to be vulnerable to others or to endure perseveringly in prayer is, as Kierkegaard tells us, 'the battlefield in which we conquer by letting God conquer'.[21] Let us remember when prayer seems dead and lifeless that this is the moment when, by keeping our attention Godward, either by prayerful reading of the Bible, or by short but sincere affective acts, or even by the sheer offering of our will to be united with his, God may not only give us his grace in ways we cannot know, but what is even more important, use our offering for others.

Relaxation as preparation for prayer

If we keep our attention in prayer directed Godwards, let this be a relaxed reflection, 'a brooding prayer', as it has sometimes been called, not a concentration of the mind which can produce strain in many ways; over-concentration in prayer may be harmful.

If we are straining in our prayer or putting a wrong emphasis on our own activity in prayer, this will probably manifest itself by pressure on our nerves, which can lead to lack of charity. There is often need for increased watchfulness when we are making some special spiritual effort, as during Lent or before or after the great festivals. We are intent on our prayer but there is too much emphasis on our own effort and on concentration, rather than on consecrated attention to God.

It is well to realize the importance of the rhythm of activity and rest, of taking in and assimilating in every stage of a spiritual life,

---

[21] Søren Kierkegaard, *Edifying Discourses*, vol. 2 (Augsburg Publishing House, 1943), 245.

and to grasp the fact that this is an essential rhythm of life. A tired mind will never meditate with true understanding; an overstrained emotion and desire will fail to be truly attentive to God and will seek relief in the vain imagination of its own heart, or will fall back into the impotence of the sense of its own inadequacy or frustration.

Today psychology has taught us a great deal about the interaction of body and soul which together make the whole person, and which work together in the actual process we call prayer. This is why I tried to emphasize that each of our faculties must be purified and unified in order that we may be ready for the Holy Spirit to bring our prayer to fruition.

There was a time when those who led a devout and spiritual life, whether secular or consecrated, were too afraid of being natural, and so relaxation as a form of preparation for prayer would not have been thought of, at least not in those terms. Rather, I am sure, we of the older generation were trained to kneel upright with folded hands and to maintain a uniform deportment throughout our times of prayer. This, I have no doubt, is a very necessary stage that most of us need to go through at one time or another. But I think it is equally true to say that most of us today have to learn, not only to *live* with tensions and fears both mental and physical, but also learn to *use* them and let them become transformed by the deepening of our prayer life in Christ. This is very important in a community or family life, because we do communicate anxiety and tension to each without knowing it. So in learning to pray there is a real need to know how to deal with physical tension within our bodies.

Some time ago a Roman Catholic psychiatrist who is also a monk, Dom Déchanet, showed us how to relax as a preparation for prayer, especially in the relation of prayer to breathing. His book, *Christian Yoga*, is very useful on this subject of relating relaxation to prayer, suggesting also how there may be a great variety of postures in prayer according to our natural temperaments.[22] Some may pray

---

[22] Jean-Marie Déchanet OSB, *Christian Yoga* (Burns & Oates, 1961).

best standing, others kneeling or prostrate on the floor or others sitting quietly relaxed in a chair with hands on the knees and head held upright. He teaches us to breathe lying on the floor in order to help us draw together all the various levels of our physical nature into a unity, and also to illustrate how the natural rhythms of our life vitally affect the way each one of us prays.

Rhythmic prayer

This leads us on to what our Orthodox brethren would call 'learning to pray always', from which has grown the widespread use of the Jesus Prayer, which is often recited aloud or internally in conjunction with breathing in and out.[23] Indeed this relation of prayer to our breathing seems to bring us naturally to the rhythmical recitation of the name of Jesus: *Jesus, Jesus, Jesus*—or perhaps just the word God, or the recitation of the Gloria or the Sanctus, or some phrase from the Our Father. Here again each one of us must find our own rhythm and interpretation of St Paul's injunction to 'pray always' (1 Thess. 5:16). But I am sure that this gentle breathing out of the Holy Name or its equivalent is the real way to prevent our prayer becoming 'compartmentalized'.

We will not go into the question of liturgy here, although of course it is the source of all our prayer, and all our private prayer must flow from it and into it, but I am sure it is the continuing prayer of the heart which goes on throughout the day almost unconsciously once the habit has been established, that brings the lives of Christians into a unity and is perhaps the answer to the age-long difficulty which the Marthas have in understanding the Marys, and vice versa.

---

[23] See Kallistos Ware, *The Power of the Name*, Fairacres Publications 43 (SLG Press, 1974, rev. 1986). A short introduction to the use of the Jesus Prayer in daily life is Bruce Batstone, *Still Listening: Sowing the Seeds of the Jesus Prayer*, Fairacres Publications 206 (SLG Press, 2023).

The use of time

My next point is about our use of time, that elusive commodity, for this too is a real part of learning to pray. The Christian has always accepted the purpose of time, for it is in time that God is magnified through the praise of his creatures and the conformity of their ways to his. It is in time that all that is evil and rebels against or falls short of the Divine Purpose is being overcome through the prayer that is *in Christo*. Religious as much as seculars share in the common lot of humanity who say, *there is no time for this or that* and yet, since we are children of time as well as of eternity, we must come to terms with it. It is a fact that even while you are reading this, what was the future earlier today has caught up with you and is now the present. The past is past and we can do nothing about it except leave it to the mercy of God, but in the sanctification of the present moment past and future can become part of our Lord's oblation and satisfaction. There is one book at least on spirituality which can never be outdated and that is de Caussade's *Abandonment to Divine Providence,* for there he shows us exactly what it means to live in the present, from moment to moment sanctifying the daily steps in time which is true prayer.[24]

For most of us there comes a point when we have to live on very short rations of time in the chronological sense. So let us once again use some words of Michel Quoist from *Prayers of Life:*

> I am not asking you tonight, Lord,
> for time to do this and then that,
> But your grace to do conscientiously,
> in the time that you give me, what you want me to do.[25]

I quoted Thomas Merton above as saying that in prayer we discover that everything has been given us in Christ. In the same

---

[24] Jean-Pierre de Caussade, *Abandonment to Divine Providence* (Cosimo, 2007). An excellent short examination of the text may be found in Barry Conaway, *The Hidden Way of Love: Jean-Pierre de Caussade's Spirituality of Abadonment*, Fairacres Publications 134 (SLG Press, 1999).
[25] Quoist, *Prayers*, 99.

context he gives us this very necessary warning: 'The trouble is that we aren't taking time to experience what we already possess.'[26]

If we really want to pray, we shall have to give time to learning its lessons. We are free to love, it is true, and every moment of the day is God's good time, but we must be realistic and give ourselves time in order to realize what we are truly seeking. Perhaps we all tend to worry too much about ourselves in prayer, when all we need to do is to be full of gratitude, praise and thanksgiving that Jesus can and will pray in us if we will let him.

What holds us back?

The basic question we should ask ourselves, I suggest, if we are aware that our prayer is not developing, is *what is holding me back?* Am I making compromises somehow, somewhere, in daily life? Am I substituting activity for growth?

The breakthrough into the riches of Christ that we already possess, so that they become living realities in our life, only happens through our complete acceptance of the Cross at that very point where it will ask most of us. There are no short-cuts to prayer unless God himself gives us the gift of infused contemplation. It is at the foot of the Cross that true prayer begins and will grow most richly and quickly as we learn to say *yes* to what God asks of us.

I should like to stress towards the end of what has been a very compressed and general consideration of learning to pray, that it is with intention that I have not tried to sketch the well-trodden stages of ascetic preparation for prayer known traditionally as the purgative, illuminative and unitive ways, at least not under those names.

I am sure it is true today, that men and women who are really desirous to pray are being led into a simpler and less formulated

---

[26] Thomas Merton, David M. Odorisio, *Thomas Merton in California* (Liturgical Press, 2024), xv.

way of contemplative prayer more quickly than the older ways of meditation generally encouraged, when the mind and the imagination played a large part in reflective consideration. But having said that, I think it is equally important that we should not go to the opposite extreme and say that no structures are needed and that we can pass into contemplative prayer at will.

Definition of contemplation

We can start out in confusion by using the word 'contemplation'. There is a natural contemplation of the artistic or reflective character who temperamentally finds formulated meditation in prayer very difficult and therefore desires merely 'to be quiet'. But this is a very different thing from infused contemplation which is a gift of God and which he bestows when and upon whom he wills. The first undoubted truth about contemplative prayer, on which all masters of the spiritual life agree, is that God gives his gifts when, where, and how he chooses. He can as easily give the gift of contemplation to a career woman or housewife as to a cloistered religious.

In contemplation God acts alone in absolute freedom. The awareness—because it is an awareness—of contemplation may come suddenly in the middle of some exercise of prayer, or even when the mind is occupied with other things. God, as it were, takes over, and the experience of union with him that follows is wholly his operation and may leave as suddenly as it came—'The Lord gave, the Lord has taken away, blessed be the name of the Lord.' But the soul is left in no doubt that it has been visited by God, and also that the whole experience is God's act and nothing of our own endeavouring. We can no more command that presence than we can delay its withdrawal. We can only adore, and know ourselves to be great sinners.

Result of contemplation

The result of such visitation is a deeper penitence in the soul, a joyous rising-up to accomplish God's will and a readiness to suffer for him. Progress in this contemplative way is best gauged by our willingness to suffer, but the soul can rarely tell at this point where or how far a person may be on the road. Indeed it is better, as I have said above, not to try to know, but only to learn to obey and to give ever more generously in self-sacrifice.

More than this I think it would be unwise to say about contemplation at this point, lest we should become self-conscious and wonder where we go from there. I would reiterate for us all that our minds, at least when we begin our prayer, must not be left *in vacuo*. Even if meditative thought or affective acts seem meaningless we must at least, as a result of our participation in the Liturgy and the Divine Office, of our reading and studying the scriptures and the works of the spiritual masters, have a 'store-cupboard' of material on which we can brood and by which our wills can be stimulated to be more truly conformed to God's will and so to manifest in our lives Christ's love and compassion to all of humanity. This is the crucial test: prayer must overflow into life, and the life must be seen to be transformed by the prayer.

The End at which we Aim

Union with God in love

We must always remember that prayer in itself is not the end of our search, though it is an essential means to union with God in love. We were made for union with God, and God himself is the goal of the journey. Prayer may indeed be the starting-point of our search and must be carried out, as we have already seen, through the dependence of a complete simplicity 'costing not less than everything'.[27] We must see this adventure of prayer not as a great good for ourselves, but principally as an invitation from our Lord who desires our ever-increasing union with him. We are to advance from glory to glory.

The ultimate danger would be if we ever reached the point in prayer of saying, *I have gone so far and that is enough.* As in the case of the Church of Laodicea: without a sense of sin or of grace misused or neglected, there would grow a lukewarmness which could indeed prevent us from going the whole way and make us stop short of that true conversion without which there can be no true union. That indeed would be not so much a Lucifer-like willed decision but much more a culpable indecision.

There must be no half-commitment, no uncertainty or hesitation between self-possession and being God-possessed, no playing safe in our Christian vocation, for it has been well said that prayer is not an easy way of getting what we want but a difficult way of becoming what God wants us to be.[28] In prayer, as in all Christian

---

[27] T. S. Eliot, 'Little Gidding' from *Four Quartets*.
[28] Gordon Clarke Chapman, *Some Say it Thundered, with a Foreword [by] Charlotte Chapman* (The Church Press, 1951), 57.

living, we have to take genuine risks, yet the blessed assurance is always ours that if we are faithful, if we harness our energies and keep our perspective right, the goal of the love of God is unlimited.

Contemplation, the life of the spirit, becomes more and more the inspiration of action, and through the long practice in the seeking of prayer and true Christian unity, the vision grows clearer and all our acts and thoughts do become more worshipful, more charged with the sense of the power and presence of God, until such time as this life *in via* is over and there will be no longer any need of prayer for, as St John says, 'We shall see him as he is' (1 John 3:2).

The underlying spiritual conflict

Perhaps we can best conclude with the question with which we began, 'Why should we pray?' Without over-simplifying, I will give you the answer in one sentence: *So that we can take our part in the underlying spiritual conflict.* This seems to me a relevant answer, because we are all being asked to give our Christian witness now, in this time and age.

Each one of us, when first taken into Christ by Baptism, was pledged 'to fight manfully under Christ's banner'.[29] Think for a while of this great conflict, the warfare of the Lord. Enlarge your minds, reach out beyond the things that are obvious and remember that this conflict is a conflict of spirit although we see it being fought out in the arena of history. It is a spiritual warfare entered upon before humankind appeared on earth. The spirit world holds the origin of those things that we know by observation. The forms of evil are sufficiently clear before our eyes, sufficiently insistent in the pain they bring into our lives and into the lives of those we love, but evil itself is a far stronger force, a power in the spirit world in direct revolt against God.

---

[29] Book of Common Prayer, 'The Ministration of Public Baptism of Infants'.

In this great conflict in the eternal order, the kingdom of God is that which is steadfast, sure, unshakeable and realized for each one of us by prayer. The presence of evil, *that* is the aggressor. Where it began is not for us to know. How it began we cannot understand. What we know is that there is the eternal holiness above and beyond all time, and the kingdom of God whose law is love and holiness, and against that there arises somewhere in the spirit world the presence of evil, the spirit of revolt.

The conflict may seem long drawn out, but the ultimate victory of the kingdom of God is certain. We are so held in by temporal conditions that we are apt to forget the eternal security of the city of God, the absolute certainty of the glorious end that shall be.

Here surely is the spirit of the Christian calling: in the warfare of God obedience is the weapon of the world's Redeemer; the sovereignty of God is that for which he stands. For religious, the vocation is first for Christ and then to give our lives in the service of redeeming love, so to let the Holy Spirit perfect Christ within us that we shall effectively carry on his great work insofar as he entrusts it to our care. Thus it is for the secular who desires to bring their life closer to God through prayer. But there needs must be the perfecting of the Christ life within: it is he who is to be prayer in us, patience in us, to be compassion and fortitude in us, to intercede in us, to be the love of God in us, the love that inspires and keeps us unflagging and generous in our response. He is the first and one and only true sacrifice. We cannot go where he has not gone or do what he has not done. Only there, where he is already, can we triumph in him. Only in proportion as we are impregnated with his spirit shall we learn something of the vision he continually saw.

Meanwhile we must learn to give ourselves with generous hearts to the warfare to which we are pledged, the particular form of warfare to which we are called by our Christian belief. Is it not our lifelong study to grow up into Christ that Christ may be formed in us, more and more in possession, filling up our narrowness with his fullness, supporting us with his strength, inflaming our hearts with his own love for us, not for ourselves alone but for those greater purposes, the spirit warfare of God against the insurgent powers of evil in the world. I recall once again words of Fr Gilbert Shaw:[30]

> *Increase, O Lord, the number who are called*
> *to seek and give both time and quietude*
> *for the work of prayer and penitence*
> *in this age of dark confusion.*

---

[30] From Fr Gilbert Shaw's unpublished papers, SLG Archive, Convent of the Incarnation, Fairacres, Oxford.

SLG PRESS PUBLICATIONS

FP1	*Prayer and the Life of Reconciliation*	Gilbert Shaw (1969)
FP2	*Aloneness not Loneliness*	Mother Mary Clare SLG (1969)
FP4	*Intercession*	Mother Mary Clare SLG (1969)
FP8	*Prayer: Extracts from the Teaching of Father Gilbert Shaw*	Gilbert Shaw (1973)
FP12	*Learning to Pray*	Mother Mary Clare SLG (1970, rev. 3/2025)
FP15	*Death, the Gateway to Life*	Gilbert Shaw (1971, 3/2024)
FP16	*The Victory of the Cross*	Dumitru Stăniloae (1970, 3/2023)
FP26	*The Message of Saint Seraphim*	Irina Gorainov (1974)
FP28	*Julian of Norwich: Four Studies to Commemorate the Sixth Centenary of the Revelations of Divine Love*	Sister Benedicta Ward SLG, Sister Eileen Mary SLG, Sister Mary Paul SLG, A. M. Allchin (1973, 3/2022)
FP43	*The Power of the Name: The Jesus Prayer in Orthodox Spirituality*	Kallistos Ware (1974)
FP46	*Prayer and Contemplation* and *Distractions are for Healing*	Robert Llewelyn (1975, rev. 4/2025)
FP48	*The Wisdom of the Desert Fathers*	trans. Sister Benedicta Ward SLG (1975)
FP50	*Letters of Saint Antony the Great*	trans. Derwas Chitty (1975, 2/2021)
FP54	*From Loneliness to Solitude*	Roland Walls (1976)
FP55	*Theology and Spirituality*	Andrew Louth (1976, rev. 1978, 3/2024)
FP61	*Kabir: The Way of Love and Paradox*	Sister Rosemary SLG (1977)
FP62	*Anselm of Canterbury: A Monastic Scholar*	Sister Benedicta Ward SLG (1973, 2/2024)
FP67	*Mary and the Mystery of the Incarnation: An Essay on the Mother of God in the Theology of Karl Barth*	Andrew Louth (1977, 2/2024)
FP68	*Trinity and Incarnation in Anglican Tradition*	A. M. Allchin (1977, rev. 2/2025)
FP70	*Facing Depression*	Gonville ffrench-Beytagh (1978, 2/2020)
FP71	*The Single Person*	Philip Welsh (1979)
FP72	*The Letters of Ammonas, Successor of St Antony*	trans. Derwas Chitty, introd. Sebastian Brock (1979, 2/2023)
FP74	*George Herbert, Priest and Poet*	Kenneth Mason (1980)
FP75	*A Study of Wisdom: Three Tracts by the Author of The Cloud of Unknowing*	trans. Clifton Wolters (1980)
FP81	*The Psalms: Prayer Book of the Bible*	Dietrich Bonhoeffer, trans. Sister Isabel SLG (1982, rev. 3/2025)
FP82	*Prayer & Holiness: The Icon of Man Renewed in God*	Dumitru Stăniloae (1982, rev. 2/2023)
FP85	*Walter Hilton: Eight Chapters on Perfection & Angels' Song*	trans. Rosemary Dorward (1983, rev. 3/2024)
FP88	*Creative Suffering*	Iulia de Beausobre (1989)
FP90	*Bringing Forth Christ: Five Feasts of the Child Jesus by St Bonaventure*	trans. Eric Doyle OFM (1984, 3/2024)
FP92	*Gentleness in John of the Cross*	Thomas Kane (1985, rev. 2/2025)
FP94	*Saint Gregory Nazianzen: Selected Poems*	trans. John McGuckin (1986, 2/2024)

FP95	The World of the Desert Fathers: Stories and Sayings from the Anonymous Series of the Apophthegmata Patrum	trans. Columba Stewart OSB (1986, 2/2020)
FP104	Growing Old with God	Timothy N. Rudd (1988, 2/2020)
FP106	Julian Reconsidered	Kenneth Leech, Sister Benedicta Ward SLG (1988/ rev. 2/2024)
FP108	The Unicorn: Meditations on the Love of God	Harry Galbraith Miller (1989)
FP109	The Creativity of Diminishment	Sister Anke (1990)
FP110	Called to be Priests	Hugh Wybrew (1989, updated 2/2024)
FP111	A Kind of Watershed: An Anglican Lay View of Sacramental Confession	Christine North (1990, updated 2/2022)
FP116	Jesus, the Living Lord	Bishop Michael Ramsey (1992)
FP120	The Monastic Letters of Saint Athanasius the Great	trans. and introd. Leslie Barnard (1994, 2/2023)
FP122	The Hidden Joy	Sister Jane SLG, ed. Dorothy Sutherland (1994)
FP124	Prayer of the Heart: An Approach to Silent Prayer and Prayer in the Night	Alexander Ryrie (1995, 3/2020)
FP126	Evelyn Underhill, Anglican Mystic: Two Centenary Essays	A. M. Allchin, Bishop Michael Ramsey (1977, rev. 4/2025)
FP127	Apostolate and the Mirrors of Paradox	Sydney Evans, ed. Andrew Linzey & Brian Horne (1996)
FP128	The Wisdom of Saint Isaac the Syrian	Sebastian Brock (1997)
FP129	Saint Thérèse of Lisieux: Her Relevance for Today	Sister Eileen Mary SLG (1997)
FP130	Expectations: Five Addresses for Those Beginning Ministry	Sister Edmée SLG (1997, 2/2024)
FP131	Scenes from Animal Life: Fables for the Enneagram Types	Waltraud Kirschke, trans. Sister Isabel SLG (1998)
FP132	Praying the Word of God: The Use of Lectio Divina	Charles Dumont OCSO (1999)
FP133	Love Unknown: Meditations on the Death and Resurrection of Jesus	John Barton (1999, 2/2024)
FP134	The Hidden Way of Love: Jean-Pierre de Caussade's Spirituality of Abandonment	Barry Conaway (1999, rev. 2/2025)
FP135	Shepherd and Servant: The Spiritual Theology of Saint Dunstan	Douglas Dales (2000)
FP137	Pilgrimage of the Heart	Sister Benedicta Ward SLG (2001)
FP138	Mixed Life	Walter Hilton, trans. Rosemary Dorward (2001, enlarged rev. 3/2024)
FP139	In the Footsteps of the Lord: The Teaching of Abba Isaiah of Scetis	John Chryssavgis, Luke Penkett (2001, 2/2023)
FP140	A Great Joy: Reflections on the Meaning of Christmas	Kenneth Mason (2001)
FP141	Bede and the Psalter	Sister Benedicta Ward SLG (2002, 2/2024)
FP142	Abhishiktananda: A Memoir of Dom Henri Le Saux	Murray Rogers, David Barton (2003)
FP143	Friendship in God: The Encounter of Evelyn Underhill & Sorella Maria of Campello	A. M. Allchin (2003, rev. 2/2025)
FP144	Christian Imagination in Poetry and Polity: Some Anglican Voices from Temple to Herbert	Bishop Rowan Williams (2004)
FP145	The Reflections of Abba Zosimas: Monk of the Palestinian Desert	trans. and introd. John Chryssavgis (2005, 3/2022)
FP146	The Gift of Theology: The Trinitarian Vision of Ann Griffiths and Elizabeth of Dijon	A. M. Allchin (2005)
FP147	Sacrifice and Spirit	Bishop Michael Ramsey (2005)
FP148	Saint John Cassian on Prayer	trans. A. M. Casiday (2006, 2/2024)
FP149	Hymns of Saint Ephrem the Syrian	trans. Mary Hansbury (2006, 2/2024)
FP150	Suffering: Why All this Suffering? What Do I Do about It?	Reinhard Körner OCD, trans. Sister Avis Mary SLG (2006)

FP151	*A True Easter: The Synod of Whitby 664 AD*	Sister Benedicta Ward SLG (2007, 2/2023)
FP152	*Prayer as Self-Offering*	Alexander Ryrie (2007)
FP153	*From Perfection to the Elixir: How George Herbert Fashioned a Famous Poem*	
		Benedick de la Mare (2008, 2/2024)
FP154	*The Jesus Prayer: Gospel Soundings*	Sister Pauline Margaret CHN (2008)
FP155	*Loving God Whatever: Through the Year with Sister Jane*	Sister Jane SLG (2006)
FP156	*Prayer and Meditation for a Sleepless Night*	
		SISTERS OF THE LOVE OF GOD (1993, 3/2024)
FP157	*Being There: Caring for the Bereaved*	John Porter (2009)
FP158	*Learn to Be at Peace: The Practice of Stillness*	Andrew Norman (2010)
FP159	*From Holy Week to Easter*	George Pattison (2010)
FP160	*Strength in Weakness: The Scandal of the Cross*	John W. Rogerson (2010)
FP161	*Augustine Baker: Frontiers of the Spirit*	Victor de Waal (2010, rev. 2/2025)
FP162	*Out of the Depths*	
		Gonville ffrench-Beytagh; epilogue Wendy Robinson (1990, 2/2010)
FP163	*God and Darkness: A Carmelite Perspective*	
		Gemma Hinricher OCD, trans. Sister Avis Mary SLG (2010)
FP164	*The Gift of Joy*	Curtis Almquist SSJE (2011)
FP165	*'I Have Called You Friends': Suggestions for the Spiritual Life Based on the Farewell Discourses of Jesus*	Reinhard Körner OCD (2012)
FP166	*Leisure*	Mother Mary Clare SLG (2012)
FP167	*Carmelite Ascent: An Introduction to Saint Teresa and Saint John of the Cross*	
		Mother Mary Clare SLG (1973, rev. 2/2012)
FP168	*Ann Griffiths and Her Writings*	Llewellyn Cumings (2012)
FP169	*The Our Father*	Sister Benedicta Ward SLG (2012)
FP171	*The Spiritual Wisdom of the Syriac Book of Steps*	Robert A. Kitchen (2013)
FP172	*The Prayer of Silence*	Alexander Ryrie (2012)
FP173	*On Tour in Byzantium: Excerpts from The Spiritual Meadow of John Moschus*	
		Ralph Martin SSM (2013)
FP174	*Monastic Life*	Bonnie Thurston (2016)
FP175	*Shall All Be Well? Reflections for Holy Week*	Graham Ward (2015)
FP176	*Solitude and Communion: Papers on the Hermit Life*	ed. A. M. Allchin (2015)
FP177	*The Prayers of Jacob of Serugh*	ed. Mary Hansbury (2015)
FP178	*The Monastic Hours of Prayer*	Sister Benedicta Ward SLG (2016)
FP179	*The Desert of the Heart: Daily Readings with the Desert Fathers*	
		trans. Sister Benedicta Ward SLG (2016)
FP180	*In Company with Christ: Lent, Palm Sunday, Good Friday & Easter to Pentecost*	
		Sister Benedicta Ward SLG (2016)
FP181	*Lazarus: Come Out! Reflections on John 11*	Bonnie Thurston (2017)
FP182	*Unknowing & Astonishment: Meditations on Faith for the Long Haul*	
		Christopher Scott (2018)
FP183	*Pondering, Praying, Preaching: Romans 8*	Bonnie Thurston (2019, 2/2021)
FP184	*Shem'on the Graceful: Discourse on the Solitary Life*	
		trans. and introd. Mary Hansbury (2020)
FP185	*God Under My Roof: Celtic Songs and Blessings*	Esther de Waal (2020)
FP186	*Journeying with the Jesus Prayer*	James F. Wellington (2020)
FP187	*Poet of the Word: Re-reading Scripture with Ephraem the Syrian*	
		Aelred Partridge OC (2020)
FP188	*Identity and Ritual*	Alan Griffiths (2021)
FP189	*River of the Spirit: The Spirituality of Simon Barrington-Ward*	Andy Lord (2021)

FP190	*Prayer and the Struggle against Evil*	John Barton, Daniel Lloyd, James Ramsay, Alexander Ryrie (2021)
FP191	*Dante's Spiritual Journey: A Reading of the Divine Comedy*	Tony Dickinson (2021)
FP192	*Jesus the Undistorted Image of God*	John Townroe (2022)
FP193	*Our Deepest Desire: Prayer, Fasting & Almsgiving in the Writings of Saint Augustine of Hippo*	Sister Susan SLG (2022)
FP194	*Lent with George Herbert*	Tony Dickinson (2022)
FP195	*Four Ways to the Cross*	Tony Dickinson (2022)
FP196	*Anselm of Canterbury, Teacher of Prayer*	Sister Benedicta Ward SLG (2022)
FP197	*With One Heart and Mind: Prayers out of Stillness*	Anthony Kemp (2023)
FP198	*Sayings of the Urban Fathers & Mothers*	James Ashdown (2023)
FP199	*Doors*	Sister Raphael SLG (2023)
FP200	*Monastic Vocation* SISTERS OF THE LOVE OF GOD,	Bishop Rowan Williams (2021)
FP201	*An Ecology of the Heart: Faith Through the Climate Crisis*	Duncan Forbes (2023)
FP202	*'In the image of the Image': Gregory of Nyssa's Opposition to Slavery*	Adam Couchman (2023)
FP203	*Gregory of Nyssa and the Sins of Asia Minor*	Jonathan Farrugia (2023)
FP204	*Discovery*	Arthur Bell (2023)
FP205	*Living Healing: the Spirituality of Leanne Payne*	Andy Lord (2023)
FP206	*Still Listening: Sowing the Seeds of the Jesus Prayer*	Bruce Batstone CJN (2023)
FP207	*Julian of Norwich: Four Essays to Commemorate 650 Years of the Revelations of Divine Love*	Bishop Graham Usher, Father Colin CSWG, Sister Elizabeth Ruth Obbard OC, Mother Hilary Crupi OJN (2023)
FP208	*TIME*	Dumitru Stăniloae, Kallistos Ware (2023)
FP209	*Pearls of Life: A Lifebelt for the Spirit*	Tony Dickinson (2024)
FP210	*The Way and the Truth and the Life: An Exploration by a Follower of the Way*	James Ramsay (2024)
FP211	*Cosmos, Crisis & Christ: Essays of Wendy Robinson*	Wendy Robinson (2024)
FP212	*Towards a Theology of Psychotherapy: The Spirituality of Wendy Robinson*	Andrew Louth (2024)
FP213	*Immersed in God and the World: Living Priestly Ministry*	Andy Lord (2024)
FP214	*The Road to Emmaus: A Sculptor's Journey through Time*	Rodney Munday (2024)
FP215	*Prayer Too Deep for Words*	Sister Edmée SLG (2024)
FP216	*The Prayers of St Isaac of Nineveh*	Sebastian Brock (2024)
FP217	*Two Medieval English Saints: Cuthbert and Alban*	Sister Benedicta Ward SLG (2024)
FP218	*Encountering the Depths*	Mother Mary Clare SLG (1981, rev. 3/2024)
FP219	*Conflict and Concord*	Sister Susan SLG, Bishop Humphrey Southern, Bronwen Neil, Sister Rosemary SLG, Sister Clare-Louise SLG (2024)
FP220	*Divine Love in the Song of Songs*	Sister Edmée SLG (2024)
FP221	*Zeal for the Faith: An Introduction to Christian-Muslim Dialogue*	Tony Dickinson (2024)
FP222	*Bernard & Abelard*	Sister Edmée SLG (2024)
FP223	*Eliot's Transitions: T. S. Eliot's Search for Identity and the Society of the Sacred Mission at Kelham Hall*	Vincent Strudwick (2024)
FP224	*Landscape, Soul and Spirit: Ecology, Prayer and Robert Macfarlane*	Andy Lord (2025)
FP225	*Our Home is in God*	John Townroe (2025)
FP226	*Our Home is in God*	John Townroe (2025)

CONTEMPLATIVE POETRY SERIES

CP1	*Amado Nervo: Poems of Faith and Doubt*	trans. John Gallas (2021)
CP2	*Anglo-Saxon Poets: The High Roof of Heaven*	trans. John Gallas (2021)
CP3	*Middle English Poets: Where Grace Grows Ever Green*	ed. John Gallas (2021)
CP4	*The Voice inside Our Home: Selected Poems*	Edward Clarke (2022)
CP5	*Women & God: Drops in the Sea of Time*	trans. and ed. John Gallas (2022)
CP6	*Gabrielle de Coignard & Vittoria Colonna: Fly Not Too High*	trans. John Gallas (2022)
CP7	*Chancing on Sanctity: Selected Poems*	James Ramsay (2022)
CP8	*Gabriela Mistral: This Far Place*	trans. John Gallas (2023)
CP9	*Henry Vaughan & George Herbert: Divine Themes and Celestial Praise*	ed. Edward Clarke (2023)
CP10	*Love Will Come with Fire: Anthology*	SISTERS OF THE LOVE OF GOD (2023)
CP11	*Touchpapers: Anthology*	coll. and trans. John Gallas (2023)
CP12	*Seasons of my Soul: Selected Poems*	Clare McKerron (2023)
CP13	*Reinhard Sorge: Take Flight to God*	trans. John Gallas (2024)
CP14	*Embertide: Encountering Saint Frideswide*	Romola Parish (2024)
CP15	*Thomas Campion: Made All of Light*	ed. and introd. Julia Craig-McFeely (2024)
CP16	*When God Hides: Selected Poems*	Joseph Evans (2025)

VESTRY GUIDES

VG1	*The Visiting Minister: How to Welcome Visiting Clergy to Your Church*	Paul Monk (2021)
VG2	*Help! No Minister! or Please Take the Service*	Paul Monk (2022)
VG3	*The Liturgy of the Eucharist: An Introductory Guide*	Paul Monk (2024)

www.slgpress.co.uk

The Sisters of the Love of God is an Anglican community of women religious living a contemplative monastic life.

To learn more about the Community and the Convent of the Incarnation at Fairacres, Oxford, see our website www.slg.org.uk.

As well as supporting those seeking to follow a vocation to the monastic life, the Community has a number of forms of association for those who feel drawn to share in the Sisters' life of prayer: Fellowship of the Love of God, Companions, Priests Associate or Oblate Sisters.

For more information email sisters@slg.org.uk or write to The Reverend Mother, Convent of the Incarnation, Parker Street, Oxford, OX4 1TB, UK.